CARRIE FISHER

Leia Forever

CARRIE FISHER

Leia Forever
BY Emily**Pullman**

FILM STARS

Volume 1

STAR WARS
EDITION

creative media
Publishing

CREATIVE MEDIA, INC.
PO Box 6270
Whittier, California 90609-6270
United States of America

Book & cover design by Joseph Dzidrums

www.creativemedia.net

First Edition: April 2017

LCCN: On File
ISBN 978-1-938438-79-0
eISBN: 978-1-938438-85-1

To Star Wars Fans
Everywhere

TABLE OF CONTENTS

*"I thought everyone had
movie star parents."*

Carrie Frances Fisher arrived in the world on the 21st of October, 1956. Her mother, Debbie Reynolds, was a beloved film star from *Singin' in the Rain*. Her father, Eddie Fisher, was a successful pop singer. The family lived in a beautiful home in Beverly Hills, California.

In true Hollywood fashion, Carrie's birth resembled a slapstick scene from a movie comedy. Aided by an anesthetic, her mother slept through the labor. Meanwhile, her father fainted in the delivery room just as she arrived in the world. Two hours later, a photographer from *Life Magazine* snapped Carrie's first official photograph.

On February 24, 1958, Debbie and Eddie welcomed a second child into their family. They named him Todd. To the outside world, the Fishers seemed like a perfect family. However, the couple split a year later when Eddie divorced his wife to marry actress Elizabeth Taylor.

Carrie was only two years when her parents' marriage ended. She and Todd remained with their mother in their Beverly Hills home. The Fisher children only saw their father sporadically from then on.

As a child, Carrie thought that her mother was the most beautiful woman in the world. She often compared herself to her mom and thought she would never measure up to her looks. The young girl felt insecure and awkward next to her glamorous parent.

Carrie knew early on that she had famous parents. Whenever she went out with her mother on an outing, fans always approached Debbie to ask for her autograph. Over time, the youngster resented sharing her mom with everyone else.

Due to her bustling career, Debbie wasn't home as much as most parents were. Sometimes the hardworking mother would come home and sleep for hours from exhaustion. Carrie and Todd often snuck into her bedroom and slept on the floor by her bed just to spend time with her.

Although Carrie yearned for more companionship with her mother, it was still more time than she had with her dad. Sometimes the youngster caught a glimpse of her father on television, and she would study the screen intently, memorizing his physical features just to feel closer to him.

A lonely girl, Carrie spent many hours with her nose buried in a book. She sought refuge in fictional worlds that existed in classic literature. Stories comforted her because they almost always ended happily. She read so much that her family nicknamed her The Bookworm.

Calling Carrie's childhood nontraditional would be an understatement. After all, the young girl and her brother grew up on movie sets. Her birthday parties took place on MGM's back lot.

In 1960, Debbie married a second time when she wed businessman Harry Karl. As it turned out, the owner of Karl's Shoe Stores had a daughter named Tina who was the same age as Carrie. The two girls became fast friends and even shared a bedroom in the family's lavish home with three swimming pools.

During her teenage years, Carrie attended Beverly Hills High School. Her classmates later described her as lovely, unaffected, and down-to-earth. She even sang in the school choir.

Carrie's mother always encouraged her to sing, stating she had a beautiful singing voice that moved her to tears. When the youngster was just 13 years old, she made her debut in her mother's nightclub act. At age 15, the teenager impressed audiences with a rich, powerful version of "Bridge over Troubled Water" by Simon & Garfunkel. Little did the young singer know that she would one day grow up to marry one-half of the American music duo.

Did You Know?

Fresh off of winning the Miss Burbank Pageant, Debbie Reynolds was just 19 years old when she scored the role of a lifetime. The teenager played Kathy Selden, the singing and dancing sweetheart who won the heart of Gene Kelly in the film classic Singin' in the Rain.

"I used to always sing 'If I Loved You' with my father."

Carrie captured her first professional acting role at age fifteen. She appeared as a debutante and chorus member in the Broadway musical *Irene* starring her mother as the title character. The musical follows an immigrant shop assistant who mingles with high society after a dame hires her to redecorate her home.

After making her Broadway debut, Carrie moved to London to attend the Royal Central School of Speech & Drama. The school offered various degrees and courses in acting, stagecraft, speech, musical theatre, writing, and teaching. Its notable alumni included Sir Laurence Olivier, Vanessa Redgrave, and Judi Dench.

Seventeen-year-old Carrie made her film debut in *Shampoo*. The mature comedy takes place in a 24-hour period on the day after Richard Nixon's presidential election. Although the teenager had a small role in the box office hit, she felt thrilled to work with Goldie Hawn, Warren Beatty, and Lee Grant.

Two years later, while on winter break from school, Carrie simultaneously auditioned for two projects. Directors George Lucas and Brian De Palma were each casting their upcoming movies. Lucas was prepping a space adventure called *Star Wars*, and De Palma was helming a horror movie entitled *Carrie*. Since both films sought a teen-age girl, they held joint auditions. Every actress would audition for both movies.

Carrie spent the first part of her tryout chatting with the directors so they could get to know her. Afterward, she went into a smaller room and read lines from each movie's script while a cameraman videotaped her. The young actress felt more comfortable reading the *Star Wars* dialogue.

Sure enough, the directors agreed. Carrie received the *Star Wars* script in the mail a few days later. George Lucas asked her to practice several scenes for a final reading. If he liked her, she would play Princess Leia, the rebellious teenager leading a revolution in space.

Carrie rehearsed scenes with her good friend Miguel Ferrer until she felt confident about her performance. When the nineteen-year-old auditioned at the reading, she acted opposite a relatively-unknown actor named Harrison Ford. Apparently, she impressed Lucas because he offered her the role a week later!

Did You Know?

Like her mother, Carrie Fisher was also 19 when she won an iconic film role, Princess Leia in Star Wars. The talented teenager beat out some notable names for the coveted part including: Cindy Williams, singer Terri Nunn, Jodie Foster, and Amy Irving.

"I'm Leia and Leia is me."

Aside from Sir Alec Guinness, who signed to play an old Jedi named Obi-Wan Kenobi, Carrie's cast members were primarily unknown actors. Fresh-faced Mark Hamill would play Luke Skywalker, the Tatooine farm boy and student of Kenobi. Meanwhile, Harrison Ford, seen in George Lucas' earlier film *American Graffiti*, rounded out the main roster as Han Solo, a cocky mercenary.

Star Wars filmed primarily in England. Upon arriving on set, Carrie worked with hairdresser Pat McDermott to create a unique look for Princess Leia. After trying 30 different designs, they selected a style with a coiled hair bun on each side of the head. The look would become an iconic hairstyle.

In *Star Wars*, Luke Skywalker sets out to rescue Princess Leia who is being held hostage by evil Darth Vader on the Imperial space station known as the Death Star. Along the way, the earnest young man meets Jedi Master Obi-Wan Kenobi and cynical pilot Han Solo, and he attempts to eliminate the evil Empire. Truthfully, no one involved in the movie knew if it would be a hit or not.

Star Wars took nearly 15 weeks to film. When production shut down, Carrie returned home to Los Angeles, unaware that the movie she had just completed would become one of the most successful of all time.

When *Star Wars* hosted its premiere months later, many expected the film to bomb. Carrie felt so nervous, she couldn't sit still during the showing. The anxious actress walked to the back of the theater, so she didn't have to watch. Eventually, her brother Todd convinced her to return to her seat by assuring her that people loved it.

To say *Star Wars* became a massive hit would be an understatement. The film was a flat-out blockbuster. Ticket lines were massively long. Retailers couldn't keep *Star Wars* toys on their shelves.

Carrie graced countless magazine covers. She hosted *Saturday Night Live*, appeared on talk shows, and attended the Oscars when *Star Wars* received a Best Picture nomination. The movie was an undeniable success, and so was Carrie Fisher.

Star Wars at the Academy Awards

Won

Best Costume Design
John Mollo

Best Film Editing
Paul Hirsch, Marcia Lucas, Richard Chew

Best Original Score
John Williams

Best Production Design
Roger Christian, John Barry, Norman Reynolds, Leslie Dilley

Best Sound Mixing
Derek Ball, Don MacDougall, Bob Minkler, Ray West

Best Visual Effects
Robert Blalack, Grant McCune, John Stears, John Dykstra, Richard Edlund

Special Achievement Academy Award
Ben Burtt

Nominated

Best Picture
Gary Kurtz

Best Actor in a Supporting Role
Alec Guinness

Best Director
George Lucas

Best Original Screenplay
George Lucas

"Good actors are travelers; they get outside of themselves and play people distant from themselves, with emotions and accents."

In 1980, Carrie co-starred in the big-screen comedy *The Blue Brothers.* Reprising their *Saturday Night Live* roles, John Belushi and Dan Aykroyd played Jake and Elwood Blues, two white boys with a whole lot of soul. The film was a modest success, earning 54 million dollars at the box office.

Later that year, Carrie starred in the eagerly-anticipated *Star Wars* sequel, *The Empire Strikes Back.* In the franchise's second installment, Princess Leia remains determined to bring down the Empire, but she also finds love with the roguish Han Solo. The sizzling chemistry between the princess and the scoundrel charmed audiences, and the duo quickly became one of cinema's all-time favorite couples.

The Empire Strikes Back marked one of the rare times when a movie sequel received greater praise than its predecessor. Audiences again flocked to the space saga featuring Luke, Leia, and Han, boosting the film to worldwide ticket sales that surpassed 450 million dollars.

The film's merchandise sales were equally impressive. Carrie as Princess Leia donned an assortment of collector's items, like lunch boxes, t-shirts, posters, dolls, mugs, Pez dispensers, trading cards, and more. On Halloween, it seemed like every female wore a Leia costume. In fact, 35 years after *Empire's* release, a *Google* poll determined that the Princess of Alderaan was the most popular costume of 2016.

Two years later, Carrie flew to New York to appear in another Broadway show. The 24-year-old portrayed the title character in the acclaimed drama, *Agnes of God*.

On May 25, 1983, Carrie returned to her royal roots when the third film in the *Star Wars* trilogy, *Return of the Jedi*, opened with great fanfare. In the epic conclusion, the Jedi, Princess, and smuggler band together once again in the hope of finally defeating Darth Vader and the Empire.

Movie fans devoured the sequel. *Return of the Jedi* grossed more money than its predecessor, and critics praised the film. It also received a Special Achievement Academy Award for Visual Effects.

On August 23, 1983, Carrie married singer/songwriter Paul Simon. The two had met on the *Star Wars* set and dated for several years.

Although the marriage ultimately lasted under a year, they remained friends for a long time afterward. In fact, Carrie became so fond of Paul's son, Harper, from his previous marriage, that she helped raised him for many years.

With the end of the *Star Wars* saga, many wondered what Carrie would do for an encore? Little did anyone realize, her greatest talent had yet to be uncovered.

Notable Film and TV Appearances

Star Wars: The Last Jedi
2017

Catastrophe
2015

Star Wars: The Force Awakens
2015

Jay and Silent Bob Strike Back
2001

Austin Powers: International Man of Mystery
1997

Soapdish
1991

When Harry Met Sally
1989

The 'Burbs
1989

Hannah and Her Sisters
1986

The Man with One Red Shoe
1985

Garbo Talks
1984

Star Wars: Episode VI - Return of the Jedi
1983

Under the Rainbow
1981

The Blues Brothers
1980

Star Wars: Episode V - The Empire Strikes Back
1980

Star Wars: Episode IV - A New Hope
1977

Shampoo
1975

"I fell in love with words."

Throughout Carrie's life, she had always suffered from severe mood swings. Sometimes she had a big personality and lit up a room. Other times, she had little energy and spent her time sleeping. She felt as if she were always riding a roller coaster, never knowing when a mood shift would occur.

To help cope with the ever-changing moods, Carrie began taking drugs and medication without her doctor's supervision. This was a dangerous decision that she later regretted for the rest of her life.

When Carrie was 24 years old, a doctor diagnosed her with Bipolar Disorder. The treatable mental illness causes extreme changes in temperament, thought, energy, and behavior. Mood shifts can last for hours, days, weeks, or even months.

For several years, Carrie refused to believe she had Bipolar Disorder despite her doctor's insistence. Many felt she was in denial about her disease. Thus, without proper medication, her mood swings continued with no relief in sight.

When Carrie was 29 years old, she nearly died of a drug overdose. Something needed to change. She checked herself into a rehabilitation center to get clean and stop taking the harmful drugs.

Carrie also admitted to herself that her doctor might be right. Perhaps, she did have Bipolar Disorder. She began receiving medical treatment for her mental illness and noticed that her moods leveled out substantially.

While Carrie recovered, she discovered her love for writing. When a publisher asked her to write a non-fiction book, the idea seemed tempting. She toyed with writing a memoir but didn't feel ready to face aspects of her past yet.

In the end, she wrote a semi-autobiographical novel based on some events in her life. Simon & Schuster published *Postcards from the Edge* in 1987. It tells the story of actress Suzanne Vale as she tries to recover from a drug overdose and moves back home to stay with her celebrity mother. The book received strong praise from *The New York Times*, *The Washington Post*, and the *Los Angeles Times*. Readers loved it, too, turning the novel into a bestseller.

Not surprisingly, Hollywood quickly gobbled up the screen rights to *Postcards from the Edge*. Oscar-winning director Mike Nichols directed the movie version for Columbia Pictures. Meryl Streep agreed to play Suzanne, while Shirley MacLaine took the mother role.

Critics and audiences embraced the big-screen version of *Postcards from the Edge*. Reviews praised the film's smart dialogue and outstanding performances. Meanwhile, the movie opened at number one at the box office. Also, Carrie earned a BAFTA nomination for Best Screenplay, and Meryl Streep received an Oscar nomination for Best Actress.

Carrie's writing credits skyrocketed after her literary success. She published additional works, the fictional novels *Surrender the Pink* and *Delusions of Grandma*. The in-demand writer also did uncredited rewrites on the movies, *Outbreak*,

The Wedding Singer, *Hook*, and *Sister Act*.

Thankfully for movie fans, Carrie still appeared in the occasional acting project. In her biggest post-*Star Wars* role, she earned great reviews as Meg Ryan's best friend in *When Harry Met Sally*. Her other film appearances included *Austin Powers: International Man of Mystery*, *Jay and Silent Bob Strike Back*, and *Hannah and Her Sisters*.

Carrie now successfully balanced a thriving writing and acting career. Soon, she would add a third role to her life.

"What I know about love, I learned from being a mother."

Carrie's favorite role occurred on July 27, 1992, when she and Creative Artists Agency agent Bryan Lourd welcomed their daughter, Billie Catherine Lourd, into their lives. The writer/actress had always wanted to be a mother. At age 11, she had even asked her mother to save her baby clothes for her future daughter.

Billie was a demanding bundle of energy whom Carrie loved dearly. A bossy young thing, she often demanded her mother's attention. "No work," "Get off the phone," and "Come play," were her favorite commands.

Although Carrie and Bryan eventually split, they maintained a healthy relationship. Billie spent two days a week with her father. The remainder of the time, mother and daughter lived together in a sprawling, three-acre, Spanish-style ranch home in Beverly Hills. They filled their eclectic home with everything from a year-round Christmas tree to a space room featuring silly *Star Wars* memorabilia. A swimming pool and tennis court highlighted the large backyard. Eventually, Debbie bought the home next door, making daily visits to see her daughter and granddaughter.

In 2008, Carrie published her autobiographical book, *Wishful Drinking*. An audio version of the piece earned her a Grammy Award nomination for Best Spoken Word Album. She, then, toured the country performing a play version of the work before opening on Broadway at Studio 54 on October 4, 2009. The hit show earned high praise and extended its run due to strong ticket sales.

The New York Times' Ben Brantley called *Wishful Drinking*, "a brut-dry, deeply funny memoir of a show."

On October 30, 2012, Disney announced that they had purchased Lucasfilm. The crown jewel of the 4-billion-dollar deal was *Star Wars*. The conglomerate announced plans to expand the movie's presence in its theme parks and release a new film in the series every four years.

Fans immediately began speculating on whether Disney might resurrect the famed trio of Luke, Leia, and Han for a new adventure. A few months later, conjecture became fact when Mark Hamill, Carrie Fisher, and Harrison Ford all signed contracts to appear in a new *Star Wars* film to be directed by J.J. Abrams.

In April of 2014, *Star Wars: The Force Awakens* began filming. Upon flying to England for the shoot, Carrie felt initially nervous when cameras began rolling and kept forgetting her lines. Eventually, though, she overcame her anxiety and settled back comfortably back into the familiar role.

Star Wars: The Force Awakens premiered in Los Angeles on December 14, 2015. Carrie felt thrilled to walk the red carpet with her daughter, Billie, who had a small role as Lieutenant Kaydel Ko Connix.

The seventh *Star Wars* movie received rave reviews. It also earned 57 million dollars on its opening night alone. *The Force Awakens* easily claimed the top spot as 2015's number one movie, and it also became the franchise's highest grossing film.

Throughout appearances promoting *The Force Awakens*, the world met Carrie's dog, Gary. The French Bulldog with the never-ending tongue was a registered therapy canine who helped the actress remain calm. He even inspired a popular *Twitter* account run by one of Carrie's fans and earned over 10,000 followers.

Carrie was enjoying a career resurgence. With the number one movie of the year and a new book on the way, she was more popular than ever.

Carrie Fisher's Bibliography

Postcards from the Edge
1987 Fiction

Surrender the Pink
1990 Fiction

Delusions of Grandma
1993 Fiction

The Best Awful There Is
2004 Fiction

Wishful Drinking
2008 Non-fiction

Shockaholic
2011 Non-fiction

The Princess Diarist
2016 Non-fiction

"I'll go to my grave as Princess Leia. In the street, they call out, 'Hey, Princess!'"

On December 23, 2016, Carrie was heading home to Los Angeles on an airplane flight from London when she went into cardiac arrest. Upon the plane's landing, paramedics rushed her to UCLA Medical Center. She died four days later at age 60. The following day, Debbie Reynolds passed away after suffering a stroke while planning her daughter's funeral.

George Lucas summarized most people's thoughts on Carrie when he said, "She was our great and powerful princess. She will be missed by all."

"Carrie was one-of-a-kind…brilliant, original," Harrison Ford told *PEOPLE Magazine*. "Funny and emotionally fearless. She lived her life, bravely…My thoughts are with her daughter Billie, her mother Debbie, her brother Todd, and her many friends. We will all miss her."

"It's never easy to lose such a vital, irreplaceable member of the family, but this is downright heartbreaking," Mark Hamill wrote on his

Facebook account. "Carrie was one-of-a-kind who belonged to us all – whether she liked it or not. She was our Princess."

All over the world, people mourned the loss of Carrie Fisher and Debbie Reynolds. In Austin, Texas, outside the Alamo Drafthouse Cinema, *Star Wars* fans raised their light sabers in Carrie's honor. Hundreds of fans swarmed Downtown Disney in Anaheim, California, for a light saber vigil. In New York City and San Francisco, people walked the streets dressed in Princess Leia costumes.

People weren't just mourning the actress who played a princess, though. They remembered a talented writer, a mental health advocate, and someone who seemed like a friend to everyone.

Although, let's be honest, no one would ever have to work hard to remember Carrie Fisher. Yes, she would live on forever through her literary and film contributions. But, more than anything, Carrie Fisher the person was unforgettable.

Carrie at The Force Awakens premiere
Kazuki Hirata / HollywoodNewsWire.net / PR Photos

Carrie at a book signing
Janet Mayer / PR Photos

Carrie, Billie, and Gary
Stills Press / PR Photos

Carrie and a Stormtrooper
Landmark / PR Photos

ESSENTIAL LINKS

Official Websites
www.carriefisher.com
www.debbiereynolds.com
www.starwars.com

Facebook
www.facebook.com/carrieffisher
www.facebook.com/thedebbiereynolds

Twitter
@carrieffisher
@DebbieReynolds1

Instagram
www.instagram.com/carriefisherofficial
www.instagram.com/garyfisher
www.instagram.com/praisethelourd

THEY ARE IN THE GALAXY FAR, FAR AWAY

A mural pays homage to David Bowie and Carrie Fisher, two stars the world lost in 2016

Creative Media Publishing has produced biographies on several inspiring personalities: *Simone Biles, Nadia Comaneci, Clayton Kershaw, Mike Trout, Yuna Kim, Shawn Johnson, Nastia Liukin, The Fierce Five, Gabby Douglas, Sutton Foster, Kelly Clarkson, Idina Menzel, Missy Franklin* and more. They've published two award-winning Young Adult novels, *Cutters Don't Cry* (Moonbeam Children's Book Award) and *Kaylee: The "What If?" Game* (Children's Literary Classic Awards). They have also produced a line of popular children's book series, including *The Creeper and the Cat, Future Presidents Club, Princess Dessabelle* and *Quinn: The Ballerina*.

www.CreativeMedia.net
@CMIPublishing

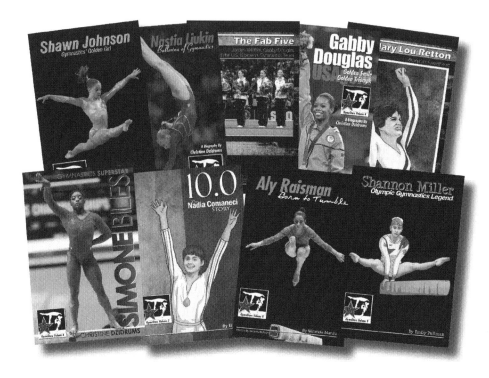

Now sports fans can learn about gymnastics' greatest stars! Americans **Shawn Johnson** and **Nastia Liukin** became the darlings of the 2008 Beijing Olympics when the fearless gymnasts collected 9 medals between them. Four years later at the 2012 London Olympics, America's **Fab Five** claimed gold in the team competition. A few days later, **Gabby Douglas** added another gold medal to her collection when she became the fourth American woman in history to win the Olympic all-around title. The *GymnStars* series reveals these gymnasts' long, arduous path to Olympic glory. *Gabby Douglas: Golden Smile, Golden Triumph* received a **2012 Moonbeam Children's Book Award**.

Our **YNot Girl** series chronicles the lives and careers of the world's most famous role models. ***Jennie Finch: Softball Superstar*** details the California native's journey from a shy youngster to softball's most famous face. In ***Kelly Clarkson: Behind Her Hazel Eyes***, young readers will find inspiration reading about the superstar's rise from a broke waitress with big dreams to becoming one of the recording industry's top musical acts. ***Missy Franklin: Swimming Sensation*** narrates the Colorado native's transformation from a talented swimming toddler to queen of the pool.

After her triumphant turn as *Thoroughly Modern Millie*, Sutton Foster charmed Broadway audiences by playing a writer, a princess, a movie star, a nightclub singer, and a Transylvania farm girl. A children's biography, **Sutton Foster: Broadway Sweetheart, TV Bunhead** details the role model's rise from a tiny ballerina to the toast of Broadway.

Idina Menzel's career has been "Defying Gravity" for years! With starring roles in *Wicked* and *Rent*, the Tony-winner filmed a recurring role on *Glee* and lent her talents to the Disney films, *Enchanted* and *Frozen*. A children's biography, **Idina Menzel: Broadway Superstar** narrates the actress' rise to fame!

Get ready to chase your dreams after reading this thrilling children's biography on *Hamilton* creator **Lin-Manuel Miranda**. A terrific source for a book report, **Lin-Manuel Miranda: Lights Up** tells the inspiring life story of the role model's transformation from a young boy with Broadway dreams to one of today's most respected artists.

Twelve-year-old Emylee Markette has felt invisible her entire life. Then one fateful afternoon, three beautiful sisters arrive in her sleepy New England town and instantly become the most popular girls at Forest Springs Middle School. To everyone's surprise, the Fay sisters befriend Emylee and welcome her into their close-knit circle. Before long, the shy loner finds herself running with the cool crowd, joining the track team and even becoming friends with her lifelong crush.

Through it all, though, Emylee's weighed down by nagging suspicions. Why were the Fay sisters so anxious to befriend her? How do they know some of her inner thoughts? What do they truly want from her?

When Emylee eventually discovers that her new friends are secretly fairies, she finds her life turned upside down yet again and must make some life-changing decisions.

Fair Youth: Emylee of Forest Springs marks the first volume in an exciting new book series.

Ashley Moore wants to know why there's never been a girl president. Before long the inspired six-year-old creates a special, girls-only club - the **Future Presidents Club**. Meet five enthusiastic young girls who are ready to change the world. *Future Presidents Club: Girls Rule* is the first book in a series about girls making a difference!

Meet **Princess Dessabelle**, a spoiled, lonely princess with a quick temper.

In *Princess Dessabelle Makes a Friend*, the lonely youngster discovers the meaning of true friendship. *Princess Dessabelle: Tennis Star* finds the pampered girl learning the importance of good sportsmanship.

Quinn the Ballerina can hardly believe it's finally performance day. She's playing her first principal role in a production of *The Sleeping Beauty*.

Yet, Quinn is also nervous. Can she really dance the challenging steps? Will people believe her as a cursed princess caught in a 100-year spell?

Join Quinn as she transforms into Princess Aurora in an exciting retelling of Tchaikovsky's *The Sleeping Beauty*. Now you can relive, or experience for the first time, one of ballet's most acclaimed works as interpreted by a 9 year old.

From the popular new series, ***Classical Reboots,*** *Rapunzel* updates the **Brothers Grimm** fairy tale with hilarious and heartbreaking results.

Rapunzel has been locked in her adoptive mother's attic for years. Just as the despondent teenager abandons hope of escaping her private prison, a mysterious tablet computer appears. Before long, Rapunzel's quirky fairy godmother, Aiko, has the conflicted young girl questioning her place in the world.

Cutters Don't Cry
2010 Moonbeam Children's Book Award Winner! In a series of raw journal entries written to her absentee father, a teenager chronicles her penchant for self-harm, a serious struggle with depression and an inability to vocally express her feelings.

Kaylee: The 'What If?' Game
"I play the 'What If?'" game all the time. It's a cruel, wicked game."

When free spirit Kaylee suffers a devastating loss, her personality turns dark as she struggles with depression and un-resolved anger. Can Kaylee repair her broken spirit, or will she remain a changed person?

Made in the USA
San Bernardino, CA
17 October 2017